SANITY IS THE FUTURE OF WEALTH

By Aaron Clarey

To Atham and Chad.

May the world never judge your forbidden love for one another. Stay brave and stunning.

Copyright © 2020 by Aaron Clarey

All rights reserved. No part of this publication may be reproduced, distributed, or transmitted in any form or by any means, including photocopying, recording, or other electronic or mechanical methods, without the prior written permission of the publisher, except in the case of brief quotations embodied in critical reviews and certain other noncommercial uses permitted by copyright law. For permission requests, write to the publisher, addressed "Attention:Aaron Clarey," at the e-mail address below.

captcapitalism@yahoo.com

Background

I intended "Sanity is the Future of Wealth" to be the single best post I had ever written. Not so much because of the quality of the writing, but because of the ideas it introduced. It explained how we will - and in some instances already have - achieved a post-scarcity world. How that effective post-scarcity world has affected our economic values and thus our happiness. But above all else, that in spite of having effectively unlimited resources and all our Earthly desires satisfied, human pettiness, jealousy, envy and greed springs eternal, and thus damns most people to a live a life of misery, anger, hatred, and envy.

But the real price humanity pays for its unlimited wealth is its sanity. Because with all of our real problems gone, and successfully smaller ones being resolved every day, human-kind focuses on increasingly pettier and pettier things that ultimately do not matter in life. And thus as small minds obsess over smaller things, said minds no longer focus on what matters most in life, becoming untethered from reality, and therefore being driven insane.

This makes the most precious commodity in our world today NOT money or wealth or materialism, but rather simple sanity. Simple sanity that can only come from common sense, intellectual honesty, critical thinking, frugality, and the maturity not to succumb to something as petty as jealousy. But given how society brainwashes people to focus on what worthless trinkets "rich people" have that they don't, or how nobody points out this amazing world of leisure we live in where nearly all of our basic needs can be taken care of with a 40 hour work week (assuming you don't screw it up with kids you can't afford or a worthless degree you can't pay back), it is no shock the small minds of society are duped into obsessing over what worthless material items they don't have. So much so to that their anger and jealousy consumes them, thus driving them insane, and thus wasting...nay...***torturing*** their one and preciously short life on this planet.

Alas, it was my intention to point out to larger minds that happiness (and therefore true wealth) would no longer be determined by how much money you had, but rather how sane you were as sanity would be a rare and fleeting commodity in a world of petty, spoiled, little minds. But ironically, *speaking of "small minds,"* when I posted it for free on my blog it received little if any traction. It was one of my least-read serious pieces. Very few people commented on it. And despite my best efforts to publicize it and get it into the "Market Place of Ideas," I failed. This great economic and philosophical epiphany - that arguably held the secret to happiness for all of humanity - went over like a fart in church. And so being the good economist I am, I did the only thing I could.

I took it down and am now making people pay for it as people do not value anything unless they suffer a price.

Still, in spite of having to pay for it, I hope you do appreciate this essay. All hubris and arrogance set aside, I truly do believe that sanity will increasingly be the main form of wealth in the foreseeable future, and therefore the main source of happiness or at least contentment. And for what token price you paid for this essay, I hope understanding this philosophy and implementing it in your life improves and enriches your life to the maximum extent possible.

Sincerely,

Aaron Clarey

I. De-Coupling Money from Wealth

Traditionally and historically money has equalled wealth. The reason why is money directly led to longer and better lives, easier lives that were more enjoyable, improved health, and an overall much higher standard of living. However, this causal relation between money and "wealth" is being asymptotically erased by the innovations and productions of capitalism. As technology advances, the economy becomes more efficient, and costs of nearly everything comes down, more and more "wealth" is put in the hands - or at least within reach - of the vast majority of people. Hunger, which plagued humanity for 99.9999% of it's existence, has been solved (so much so "obesity" is more of a problem now). Diseases that would have killed or otherwise crippled you, eliminated. Clothing and shelter are effectively guaranteed rights amongst the first world. And transportation across the globe is available to anyone, allowing you to travel to far away lands that kings a mere 500 years ago could only have dreamed of.

Matter of fact, economics and technology has made so many people wealthy, what we delineate between "rich" and "poor," or "luxury" and "common" goods, is often truly minor, minute, and petty.

• My 2008 Kia Rio did 99% of everything a Ferrari does. It provided me with quick, safe, reliable transportation while protecting me from the elements.

• The Subway sandwich I ate last week provided me just as a nutritious, healthy, caloric meal as the $100 sushi dinner Mr. McSnootySnootSnoots had on the Las Vegas Strip.

• My Savers and Goodwill clothes provide me just as much warmth and protection from the elements as a Harvard blue blood trustfund baby's wardrobe from Christian Dior.

• And my old, low-end smart phone connects to the internet, with 100% the functionality as Tina-The-Suburbanite-Princess's latest and greatest $5,000 Iphone 3907Xi-Tx-1.

And when you put it in the ultimate context, unless you have a disease or bad genetics, you will have the same exact life-expectancy on this planet as Bill Gates, Warren Buffet, George Soros, and Jeff Bezos even if you only have 1/1,000,000th their financial wealth. Just ask Steve Jobs how much billions of dollars-worth in "wealth" actually improved the inevitable enjoyment and quality of his life...which you can't because he's dead. Therefore, I think the focus should not be on how much more money "Bob" nominally has than "Billy," but how Billy enjoys a standard of living 98% of what Bob does with only 10% of the money.

II. What Happens Post-Unlimited Wealth?

But what would happen if the economy ever reached that utopian level of unlimited production? What if armies of human-serving robots slaved away making every human's material wish and desire come true? A world where we all had Ferrari's, we all ate sushi, we all shopped a Christian Dior, and the only thing that determined who was "wealthier" was life expectancy?

Well, one would theorize the most pressing political issue of all time would be resolved - income inequality. The democrats', socialists' and communists' dream of total income equality would be achieved and they would cease their advocation of parasiting off of the production of others. Right and left, producers and parasites, capitalists and socialists would no longer be at each other's throats. Matter of fact, politics would cease to exist because all of history's politics has merely been one group of people wanting what others had. You never know, conservatives and liberals might even get to know each other personally, resulting in the Ben Shapiro's of the world marrying the Ocasio Cortezes. Of course, I don't think that's going to happen, but what would ultimately happen is a cessation of war, theft, greed, and envy. People would have no need, nor desire to live off of others. People would not have to strive at all for what they have. And a truly utopian, "perfect world" would exist, all because wealth would be unlimited.

Of course, this pure, 100% world of parity is never going to happen. In part because somebody is always going to be jealous of someone over something. But also because of the asymptotic approach to this ideal world is mathematically impossible to reach - there will always be somebody who has it slightly better off than others. But this is the point I was trying to make earlier. I would argue we are already (mostly) there. Rather than looking at today and the paltry "inequalities" we face, consider the amazing closure of life expectancy gaps, hunger gaps, homelessness, and illness we've achieved in the past 500 years. Yes, that Rat Bastard Bob has more than Poor Person Pete, but Pete is not dying of scurvy and lice. He's just driving a Chevy and not a BMW.

If you look at it this way there's a lot of hope and happiness to have in humanity. Matter of fact, if you really think about it, we effectively have unlimited wealth today. But it takes a particularly wise, ponderous, and philosophical person to realize this fact. One who is not obsessed about materialism or is jealous of what others have, but is happy for the freedom and ease of life he's got. We call these people "minimalists" and I would argue they have the true and correct philosophical approach to understanding wealth.

Minimalists have the ability to appreciate the amazing standards of living nearly everyone enjoys today. They are also capable of appreciating the amazing levels of effective wealth they enjoy on the small token amount of money they have. Key to all of this, however, is that they are not materialists and they are not jealous of others who have more. But key to that zen-level epiphany is to realize the only thing in the world that matters is other humans. Minimalists appreciate the company, conversation, interaction and love of their fellow man above all material things because they realize while a Ferrari is a really nice car, it is finite. It can only do so much. The human mind (be it a friend's, a child's, a spouse's, or a colleague's) is unlimited in its potential, and therefore its enjoyment. It is the truest source of happiness and enjoyment in life. But where the fiscal minimalism comes in is in the fact that humans have another huge advantage - they cost you nothing. They are free. And so if you can appreciate humans for what they are, all you really need in life is food, clothing, shelter, and others, and you truly don't care if others have materially more than you.

There's just one tinsy, winsy problem when it comes to minimalism.

The vast majority of people are not minimalists. The majority of people are petty, low-brow, low-IQ, sad, materialistic and jealous creatures as they've always been for all of human history. And since they're not minimalists they are going to face some horrific problems. Not only in today's world, but even the perfect future utopian world humanity is damned to face. And when that happens the truest form of wealth will no longer be money, investments, or material things, but pure and simple sanity.

III. Forever Lazy = Forever Envious = Forever Inferior

The problem with being a leftist is that AT MOST you will only achieve half of what you want.Let me explain what I mean by that.At their core leftists are lazy. They do not want to work. They do not want to toil. They fear labor more than anything else in the world. But just as they are lazy, they are equally egotistical. They are equally envious. They CANNOT stand being inferior. They cannot stand being less of a person than others. If Bob has a nickel more more money than they do, then they are envious of Bob. If Jill has a better job than they do, then Jill should pay more in taxes. And if Frank saved up more money in his 401k, then Frank was "privileged" rat bastard.

However, leftists are not simply envious of other people's money and wealth. They are envious of everything. Looks, grades, intelligence, creativity, beauty, talent, friends, sex, popularity, nuclear families, even things as petty as height. If somebody is simply superior in some way or another to a leftist, it drives the leftist green with envy.

The problem for the leftist is that, unlike money, things like skills, looks, beauty, intelligence, bench-press gains, talent, friends, love, sex, etc., cannot be confiscated and redistributed. When I transform my time into money by providing labor, I have now converted that time into a tangible, physical item that leftists can vote to tax and take for themselves. But what if I practice years on end to become a great guitar player? What if that great guitar playing was coupled with religiously attending the gym? And in doing both what if I am able to swoon a hot woman into becoming my wife? And in doing so we have a strong marriage and relationship, resulting in a stable nuclear family for our children? And what if my talent is so good, it earns me a living where I can afford to take my kids traveling to national parks?

How exactly do leftists confiscate and tax that?

One could argue that leftists should hit the gym themselves, dedicate themselves to learning a skill and craft, hone that craft into a profitable venture, and then attract a hot wife for themselves. But again, I cannot emphasize this enough - LEFTIST FEAR WORK ABOVE EVERYTHING ELSE. They are not going to work as hard, put forth the effort, or put in the toil to achieve excellence and accomplishment, no matter how rewarding it might be. Laziness is the NUMBER ONE TRAIT that determines all their actions and it damns them to being inferior to any person simply willing to do the work. Therefore, leftists face an impossible quandary. On one hand laziness is hardwired into their genetic code. On the other hand they cannot stand being inferior. And while they can steal people's money through socialism and taxation - making them equal economically - the rest of LITERALLY EVERYTHING ELSE THAT MATTERS IN LIFE they cannot.

Love

Beauty

Talent

Happiness

Success

Pride

Accomplishments

Excellence

Sex

Strength

Creativity

and

Looks

All of those things are earned through hard work, dedication, effort, and toil, and CANNOT be stolen from the individual and given to a leftist. And these non-financial successes of other people constantly remind leftists of their inferiority and laziness, and there's not a thing they can do about it because leftists are completely controlled and crippled by their laziness.

So what is a leftist to do?

Well they're going to do three things. And in their minds doing these three things will not only metaphorically "redistribute" everybody else's non-financial traits accomplishments to them, but make these leftists equal, nay, SUPERIOR to everyone else in the world

Leftists will:

1. Redefine excellence, accomplishment, and achievement.

2. Irrationally and falsely value traits

3. Participate wholly in professional victimhood.

IV. Redefining Excellence, Accomplishment, and Achievement

The goal of eliminating "excellence" or "greatness" is very simple - to destroy objective standards that measure and prove superiority. In eliminating the concept of something being "the best" or "great" or "excellent" of "better" there's no way to prove something superior, and thus also something inferior. So without these objective standards, leftists in their little warped minds believe they can essentially, not so much "redistribute" beauty, strength, or superiority, but make it so they are no longer provably inferior via these non-financial measures. The shorter version - lying to themselves protects their feelings.

You can see this in nearly every non-economic facet of leftist politics.

We don't keep score at school games any more.

We eliminate the valedictorian and salutatorian

We eliminate GPA's.

Participation trophies.

EQ being promoted over IQ.

The "fat acceptance movement" where large (and most definitely leftist) women actually believe "big is beautiful."

Soyboys who think their male-feminist politics will make up for the fact they're noodle-armed pussies.

"Toxic Masculinty" where ACTUAL masculine achievement, competition, and superiority is considered "bad."

Awards, such as the Nobel Peace Prize or Oscars, that certainly do NOT go to the best, but who is most politically correct.

Modern art that is completely void of talent, but has the approved political message and end up in museums.

Rare talented successful artists who make it, but whose superior skills are dismissed as being a "sell out."

Truly stupid people who went $150,000 into debt for completely worthless degrees, ACTUALLY THINKING THEY'RE SMART.

And then the very feminist, Oprah-esque concept that if you simply have a vagina between you legs then you're all "brilliant, wonderful, amazing, empowered, courageous brave" people, when in reality you're just one of the tens of millions of VERY, ORDINARY, COMMON women with worthless degrees, student loans, poor job prospects, pear-shaped bodies, and nothing truly "amazing" about you.

It would be funny if it wasn't so sad how pervasive, universally-accepted, and promoted these outright lies are among our institutions and society. You almost have to tip your hat to the leftists in just how successful they've been in getting most of society to redefine what is excellence, greatness, achievement, and accomplishment. Regardless, with these concepts erased from society leftists can pretend that are no longer "inferior."

V. Irrationally Valuing Traits

The goal here is even simpler than redefining excellence. Leftists wish to put value, perhaps all their value in traits because traits are things you are born with. You do not earn them. You don't have to work for them.

For example, as mentioned before, women put an insane and irrational amount of value on being female. There's certainly nothing wrong with being female, but there's nothing morally right or superior about it either. It simply is what it is.

Race is also obviously in this category where leftists obsess about people's race and skin color, irrationally placing value (or hatred and envy) on a person because of the color of his skin and not the content of his character.

But the rabbit hole of traits goes much further than mere sex and race. It goes into any kind of trait you have, even ones you can make up or "identify with."

Sexuality and the 31 flavors of gender are a perfect example of this. Yes, there certainly are non-binary genders, normally homosexual and bi, I will even go so far as to say trans. But the 31 flavors of gender that were made up this past week are complete bogus and only serve the purpose of giving laughably pathetic people some kind of "faux value" in their otherwise completely pointless lives. You're not going to find a gainfully employed engineer, who volunteers at the Shriners, and thoroughly enjoys fishing claiming he's a "Polymorphous Aporagender Sapio Sexual." But you will find a lazy, millennial liberal arts student who's failing his remedial classes in community college who does. It's the immediate conferment of value with absolutely no work that makes these made-up identities so tempting for accomplishmentless leftists.

Another example - religion. Religion can be considered a trait because you simply "believe" it and you therefore are it. It takes no work, it takes no effort, but in the lazy hypocrite's mind he or she now has "value" in being a "Christian" or a "Jew" or a "Muslim."

But religion goes well beyond that.

Do not view religion as one of the traditional, classical religions of the world. View it as a leftist would. View it as merely a belief or something you "identify with." A cause or a purpose. A crusade or a moral position. And when you view religion through the lens of a leftist, you'll see that ANY kind of crusade or cause can become a religion. You just have to "identify" with it.

Did any of you have the high school vegan kid who believed so just so she could get attention?

What about the token, trench-coat wearing anarchist or communist? Was he there too?

How many vegetarians did you meet in college?

Environmentalists?

And after college how many of you cool hipster 20 somethings all started to claim you were Organic?

Fair trade?

Gluten free?

Soy only?

Free Range?

Bragging about your Carbon Foot Print?

Against Nuclear Arms?

And yes, yes, I know. You're all "Feminists."

The point is that like a religion, political causes or positions are just as easy to join and also require no effort or work. And most leftists today, all they have is their politics. It's truly sad to be driving down the road and you see the Prius covered in every conceivable leftist bumper sticker. Not because a bumper sticker-clad Prius is sad, but that it's proof the 48 year old woman driving it has LITERALLY NOTHING ELSE OF VALUE IN HER LIFE. No husband. No real career. No children. No love. No sex. No physical health. Still, in her mind, that life is preferable. At least she didn't have to work hard or achieve something of value to get those bumper stickers and that used Prius.

And then there's mental illness…..orrrrrr claiming you have one.

Yes, there are people who do indeed suffer from real and legitimate mental illnesses. But do not tell me the millions of millennials who "magically" all of the sudden got "Autism," "Aspergers," "Depression," "Dyslexia" and (my all time favorite) "Social Anxiety Disorder" are 100% legitimate cases instead of lazy kids. They are merely "value-whoring" for sympathy and attention, not to mention an excuse as to why they can't pass Pre-Pre-Introductory-Remedial Algebra. Faking a mental illness doesn't necessarily mean you're a rank Marxist, demanding land distribution tomorrow. But given the amount of people who can't go 30 seconds without mentioning they have a mental illness because they wear it like a badge of honor, it's painfully clear people are faking the trait of mental illness to get effortless value in their otherwise pathetic lives.

There are other examples, but the sad fact is the left has had some measure of success in getting some of society to actually believe their traits have value. For example, I was teaching a finance class and black female student of mine said in a classroom discussion "As a black female, I just think..." I didn't listen to what she said afterwards and I didn't care, because I couldn't possibly fathom how a person's race or gender would have any bearing on the tax treatment of Roth IRA's. There was another student who said her preferred pronouns were "her and she" which again grated me like Henry Bear from the Warner Brothers cartoon because her gender and preferred pronouns truly hold no value to either her or society. What's worse is I don't think these people were consciously malicious or intentional, taking faux value in their races or genders. They were successfully brainwashed to actually think their opinions carried more weight simply because they were born X or Y. Which means it's not only leftists who will consciously rush to take value in their traits, but just plain stupid people as well.

VI. The Professional Victim Whores

Then there's the professional victim whores. Here it's pretty transparent of what the left is trying to do. Claim they are oppressed or disadvantaged somehow because of a trait, and therefore are entitled to preferential treatment, other people's money, and other such goodies. While there is a financial redistribution incentive, there is also a non-financial incentive in that if you actually believe you're a victim, you can then forgive your laziness, sloth, and lack of trying in life. So if a leftist can claim he or she has a disability or is some how oppressed or discriminated against, then it's not their fault. It's society's fault!

Women don't make as much as men not because they major in worthless degrees, don't put in as many hours, and take off more time. No, it's "sexism."

Minorities are poorer than whites, not because they have more kids, also choose poorer majors, and commit more crime. Not, it's "racism." (BTW ignore Asians. They don't count as a minority).

And I can't pass my Remedial Reading Class at Durpydork Community College because I'm lazy and don't want to study. No, I have a "learning disability." BTW, give me a scholarship, special tutoring, and extra time to finish my final.

What is particularly disgusting about this breed of liberal is how they hide behind their race, sex, gender, or any other trait, thereby giving those with that same trait a bad name. But once again, you need to realize that leftists are completely and totally driven by LAZINESS above all else. They will use whatever trait they can, faking mental illnesses, falsely claiming they are a victim, as long as it prevents them from having to try in life and work. And damn which group of people it disparages, it's more important to the leftist that their fake victimhood excuses their laziness.

When you combine these three "tactics - Redefining Excellence, Placing Value in Traits, and Victim Whoring - the leftist creates in their mind (and to a certain extent society) a world where they:

1. Are just as good as everybody else, perhaps even superior.

2. Have agency, purpose, and value in life

3. Never had to work for it and, above all else,

4. Any failure or inability on their part to be on par with the rest of society is explain away by victimhood/disability

They feel no guilt. They feel no shame. And in

addition to money, they've effectively (in their minds anyway) been able to also redistribute all non-financial performance within the human race. It is, and will go down in history as, the greatest performance of mental gymnastics of all time.

The question is, will it stick?

VII. But At What Cost?

The leftists might think they're clever. They might think they've redefined reality. And they've certainly been successful in voting to get other people's money. But in the end they've fooled no one but themselves. Because in the end they are not living in reality. Oh sure, government, media, universities, women's magazines, and other societal institutions will pay leftists lip service, falsely confirming their delusions are real. And oh sure, they may be completely successful in getting 60% of other people's income. But that's not the real world. The real world doesn't give a damn about your made up mental illness, your made up quadropansexual gender, the fact you're Hispanic, or that you have a worthless "Doctorate in Sociology." And when you pit your delusions, your lies, and your entirely fabricated lives against the real world, the real world is going to absolutely and mercilessly destroy you, causing you untold amounts of pain, agony, suffering, and misery. And if you don't admit you're wrong and living a lie, the end result is guaranteed to be insanity.

First, there's "The Reality Principle." The Reality Principle is that the further removed your decisions are from reality, the less effective they will be. For example most sane, conservative or at least logical people will conclude that majoring in Women's Studies is a stupid idea. There's no employment prospects with the degree. You will waste at least 4 years of your youth learning utterly worthless faux philosophical slop. You'll go $75,000 into debt on top of it. And you'll likely come out hating men in the end.

But to a leftist their laziness blinds them to ALL of these horrific and life-damaging consequences. NONE of these real world factors enter into their decision. All that matters is what they want and that they don't have to work to get it. And so young Amy wastes $125,000 of her parents money and 6 years of her youth getting a Masters in Women's Studies. Her life is at best crippled as she can't pay off her student loans, has a troubled love life, seethes at the Patriarchy hourly, and blames all of her failures on men. She'll never admit she's wrong, but just as rock beats scissors, reality beats delusional women's studies major, and Amy's life is effectively over. She's forever poor. Forever panhandling for government grants. She'll never experience love. And instead of happiness, laughter, and joy, she's full of anger, jealousy, resentment, and hate.

Of course The Reality Principle doesn't just apply to women's studies majors, but anybody who lacks the courage to base their decisions in the real world. And leftists are epitomally defined by that.

You think "Big is Beautiful?"

You think you're poor because of "ists' and "isms?"

You think you have ADHD?

You think you're quadrohypersapiosexual?

You think "the man" is keeping you down?

You keep thinking those things. Reality will guarantee you the same failed fate as Amy, with an added dose of insanity.

Second, the costs of living a lie.

Whether deep down inside you believe it or not, there are insane costs and consequences to living a lie. Namely, you have to keep it up. And it's one thing if you tell a girl you're dating you make $80,000 when you only in fact make $60,000. But it's another thing if you lie to yourself about having a mental illness, your sexuality, or that your problems are caused by other people and not you.

Take for example Seattle city council member, Larry Gossett.

Larry will be most known for claiming that spraying the feces adorned sidewalks in Seattle would be seen as "racist" because the hoses might remind some older black citizens of being blasted by fire hoses back in the civil rights era.

Let me ask you this. How happy can Larry Gossett possibly be if he sees racism in everything?

Here you have a SUCCESSFUL leftist. One of the few to get a government job, bought and paid for by espousing taking other people's money. If I pulled off that trick as a leftist I would be quietly jumping for joy that I avoided a life of work with this cushy gig. But he honestly believes he's oppressed. He honestly believes the white man is keeping him down. And it's because his past life was not so easy. Of course, could it be because the man was a lazy leftist who has never worked for a living? Going from one non-profit job to another activist job, never parking his fat ass in an accounting or auto mechanic program? No, it's all "racism." It's all "whitey's fault." Alas, even a successful leftist can't be happy because they're living a lie.

And forget blaming other people for your mistakes. I can't even possibly begin to imagine the price a leftist pays when they lie to themselves about their sexuality or their mental health. Oh sure, you get popularity in high school claiming you're "pansexual." Oh sure, you get a taxpayer scholarship if you claim you have the Aspergers. But if you aren't these things and keep it up for a decade, what demons torture you hourly for the rest of your days until you're dead? Worse, what if this is the only thing of value you have in life? I sure hope a life of taking prescribed drugs for a fake case of depression or sleeping with a sex you're not attracted to was worth being called "amazing" and "brave" by the government and some equally worthless people obsessed with identity politics.

And finally, deep down inside even leftists don't believe their own BS.

I am completely convinced that no matter how adamant a person is, no matter how hard they try to believe their own lies, deep down inside every leftist knows EXACTLY what they're doing. They know that "big is not beautiful," they know they aren't hypochondriac sexual, they know they don't have Social Anxiety, they know it isn't "The Patriarchy" or "Whitey" holding them down, and they know it isn't the 1% or "the Man" holding them back. In their heart of hearts they know that at their core they are lazy. They are worthless, pointless, productionless, inferior people who offer nothing of value. But they are so crippled by the fear of a regular 50 years of 9-5, they'd rather live delusional lies, no matter how much it destroys them. And if you don't think leftists suffer painful and mentally insane lives, you think they're all celebrating and enjoying life living off of your tax dollars, just look at your stereotypical leftists today and honestly ask yourself how happy can they possibly be?

Your millennial soyboy "male feminists" who actually

think agreeing with women and their politics will get them laid. Too afraid to hit the gym, they are RELIEVED merely spouting leftist talking points should get them into bed with scores of women. But not only do many of these men become 40 year old virgins, what few women they sleep with are physically revolting and incapable of marriage. The insanity these soyboys must face, doing exactly what they were told for decades, only to see women run off with the evil "toxic masculinity" bad boy blue collar worker, must be infuriating. That pain is only trumped by a special pain reserved for men - never getting laid.

Your soyboy female counterpart - Generation Spinster. Leftist women were actually convinced, actually fooled into thinking that working and paying taxes was more fun than the love and compassion of a husband and children. And not only did we fool leftist women into thinking work and taxes were preferable to love and family, we got them to go into unrepayable levels of debt for laughably stupid degrees. Yes, yes, I know, I know. We've all heard it before. "you're all strong independent women who don't need no man fish bicycle trademark." Meanwhile, I can guarantee you all these proud, strong, independent leftist women cry themselves to sleep over boxes of wine because no man will marry them. Of course, they could always go after those politically-agreeable and sensitive soyboys...on second thought, never mind. Here's another tissue sweetheart. Pour yourself another glass of Franzia.

Borrowing from Larry Gossett, how many millions of poor minorities have equally wasted their lives stewing in hatred and bigotry, instead of just getting their act together, majoring in Engineering, waiting till they were married to have kids, and simply voting for lower taxes and economic growth? How many generations of leftist minorities were not only lost to poverty, but a life of anger, helplessness, and hopelessness because it was easier to "blame whitey" and vote democrat than just go and become a master electrician? The amount of pain and insanity generations of minorities have suffered I can't even begin to fathom. I can't imagine what it would be like to vote for decades for a promised solution that never freaking comes. But I can tell you this. Such an existence most certainly would drive you insane.

Speaking of being lied to your entire life, the millennials anyone? Millions of plastic surgeons had to be hired to reconstruct the millennials' throats all so they could swallow more leftist Kool-aid than any generation before them. They followed the leftist doctrine to the letter, borrowing trillions in student loans, wasting their lives away in academia, thinking their politics and organic eating habits actually held value in the real world. Now, well into their 30's they're living at home, will forever be in debt, will have to work till they die, think they have mental disorders, and for the most part are a failed generation. But here's the real kicker. They were so THOROUGHLY brainwashed that in spite of the painful empirical proof they were dead wrong about...well...everything, they still think they know better. It must drive them mad, every day, that what their parents, teachers, and Obamian-leftist politicians promised them was never delivered. Don't worry millennials. Just another 40 years before it's all over.

And speaking of millennials, what about all of the kids and adults with ADHD, ADD, Asperger's, Autism, Social Anxiety, and Depression? I'm not talking the three of them who legitimately have those mental conditions. I'm talking the 10s of millions of the other people who are faking it for attention, politics, faux agency and government handouts. If at any time you get agitated at yet another 19 year old who claims he can't work or go to school because he has "Autism" or "Social Anxiety" imagine first what painful insanity he must suffer everyday. His parents, teachers, and counselors lied to him about having a mental illness. Then wonder what damage the drugs he's taking does to his brain. THEN wonder what the long term mental consequences are of not only faking a mental illness, but taking decades worth of unnecessary drugs. I'll leave you with Exhibit A, another "successful leftist" that used mental disability to garner agency, value, and worth.

And finally, leftists who believe they are a made up gender.

Again, if a person is so lazy, so fearful of work, that they're willing to fake being a made-up gender just to get attention at school or praise from the internet, you might find it hypocritical, you might it insulting, but just imagine their sex life. At best there is none and it really is just a college girl using it as an excuse not to have sex or garner attention on Facebook. But for the true believers who go so far as to sleep with a sex they don't find attractive, or mutilate their genitalia, what does that do to your psychology? Additionally, while the current zeitgeist is to poo-poo sex, sex is one of - if not "the most"- important part of people's lives. Healthy people have healthy sex lives, gay, straight, bi, or not. But if you're FAKING IT for attention, politics, faux agency, and purpose, being "trans" or "balbausaursexual" when you're not will most definitely leave a mark.

I could go on.

Girls who self-mutilate their bodies with an overabundance of tattoos, piercings and ear gauges. Talentless artists who panhandle their entire lives for government endowments. People who become priests or priestesses of cults. Career activists who never achieve anything in life. Hippies and their healing crystals. The list is nearly endless of lazy leftists trying anything and everything to avoid work, rigor, toil, and labor. But do not be fooled. It does not come without a price. These leftists waste their lives. Their one and only brief finite shot at this universe is "blip" and gone. But what makes it worse is not only are their lives wasted, it's spent in the penury of being insane.

And I do mean that. They are insane.

VIII. Sanity as Wealth

The problem the left faces is that they're going to get what they want. Either through actual socialism where wealth is forcibly redistributed today, or through advances in technology that allows for unlimited wealth tomorrow. I argue that we are already at the point of effective, though imperfect, unlimited wealth, and we're merely haggling over Kia's vs. Ferrari's, sushi over Chipotle. But regardless of the point we're actually at, it is vital you realize that resolving income inequality only removes INCOME inequality from society.

It leaves EVERY OTHER ASPECT, FACET, AND VALUE of life and humanity on the table.

Beauty.

Strength.

Talent.

Skill.

Excellence.

Sex.

Creativity.

Love.

Pride.

Achievement.

Accomplishment.

Friendship.

Happiness.

EVERYTHING. *Only money* has been removed.

This introduces a very interesting truism about humanity. That the vast majority of value in our lives is not exchanged through money, but via humans voluntarily bartering their time, attention, and excellence with one another. I would argue this has always been the case about humanity/economics - where monetary exchange, though necessary, only accounted for a small minority of the total value of the human experience. But with income inequality gone, with wealth unlimited, THE ONLY THING remaining is the value of human interaction. But it can't just be "any" human interaction. It's going to have to be valuable, quality, and sought-after human interaction. And this will pose a problem for leftists.

For example, if we are in a truly utopian world, I'm not going to waste my time listening to the low-grade shit of Margaret Cho. I'm going to spend my time listening to the high-grade value of Victor Borge.

If we are in a utopian world, I am not going to watch the derivative "meh-ness" of Ocean's 8, I'm going to watch the great classic, The Great Escape.

And if we are in a utopian world, I am not going to waste my time chasing after hairy-armpitted, liberal, fat chicks. I'm chasing after girls with big tits, a nice demeanor, a tight ass, libertarian politics, a motorcycle, bad decision making skills, and a degree in engineering.

And here's the kicker - so will everybody else.

This presents the leftists a quandary. If they truly want to live and enjoy a good life, then they're going to have to work for it. Unlimited wealth be damned, you're not going to get a hot chick to sleep with you unless you spent some time at the gym and developed some mean salsa dancing skills on the side. You're not going to get a hot guy to marry you unless you also hit the gym and knock it off with your common, boring, unoriginal feminist nagging. And if you want to have cool, smart, fun and engaging friends, well then you better study up on some interesting philosophy, develop a craft or a trade, learn history, or dedicate yourself to self-improvement. You have to make your time, your value as a human being, valuable to others.

Sadly, most leftists are simply incapable of doing this.

When given the choice of putting forth the effort to make oneself a very valuable human being, the majority of people, when given unlimited wealth, will choose instead the path of laziness, sloth, and worthlessness. Human nature being what it is, the majority of people will choose "The Path of the Leftist" because the amount of effort, time, toil and labor it takes to become a quality human being is too much for them. Once again, laziness springs eternal, determines all, and is your lord god almighty. And I predict the majority of people will just grow fat, lazy, pointless, and meaningless.

Unfortunately, jealousy and envy also spring eternal. These leftists or "lazyists" (since there would technically be no politics in the future) will not sit idly by watching other humans grow superior to them. And since they can't tax them and "redistribute excellence," or force cool people to hang out with them, or pretty people to have sex with them, these lazyists will engage in those same insane mental acrobatics of self-delusion, lies, fake value, and "anti-excellence" highlighted before. And also as highlighted before, this path has a predictable end - misery, hate, sadness, and ultimately, insanity.

The question is what percent of a future society will

unlimited wealth drive insane? I would argue 90% because I'm a misanthrope. Others might argue 50% as today roughly half our population votes left. But it is not so much what nominal percentage equilibrium point of sanity a future society will inevitably settle on, as much as it is that it will be an increasing percentage. Remember that misery loves company, and like The Borg, the lazyists of society will insist you join them because they cannot stand the fact you're enjoying a better life than them. And this never-ending assault on sanity will make sanity a rarer and rarer commodity.

But what is "sanity?" What role would sanity play in a future society?

While you might be tempted to think that wealth in an future "unlimited wealth society" would be the quality and caliber of humans you spend your time with, you wouldn't be wrong, but there is a subtle nuance. Being sane is what causes you to be a higher quality human in the first place. Being sane and accepting the reality that you need to improve yourself as a human in order to get other quality humans to spend time with you is the cause of your enjoyable life. I would also argue that sanity protects you from the insanity and misery the rest of society suffers because you won't be wasting your tortured life confused and angry as to why you're so miserable because...well...you're sane. So while all your food, clothing, and shelter is bought and paid for, and your colleagues, lovers, family, and friends are all quality human beings, it is sanity that is the truest form of wealth simply because sanity is what made this all possible, and will thusly make you happy. And happiness in a miserable society is the only true form of wealth.

IX. The Future is Now!

And thus is our world today.

We may not be in a truly, pure 100% unlimited wealth world. And our current day "lazyists" may only account for 50% of the voting population. But there is a clear and distinct difference in today's society between the have's and have-not's when it comes to sanity.

On one hand you have the leftists. The single moms with 7 different kids from 6 different fathers who will never have a husband, but will have a government check to cuddle up next to on those cold nights. Feminist-careerist women who love their degrees more than their children, their careers more than their non-existent husbands, and will go to their grave with their cats and their MBA's. The know-it-all Millennials whose lives were ruined by the socialist professors and colleges they still swear ideological allegiance to today. The physically repugnant soyboys stuck in their basements, jerking off to porn, thinking being nice and voting for Hillary was going to get them laid. The tatted up, "big is beautiful" equally repugnant BBW's who lie to themselves daily, screaming "THEY DON"T NEED A MAN" when that is all they desperately want at night. The Larry Gossett's of the world whose entire lives are ruined by race as that is all they can see. The otherwise mentally healthy people, who are no longer mentally healthy because they we're lied to about their non-existent case of Anxiety or Autism. The otherwise straight person who claims to be ferrousoxidesexual because it garners them attention, completely disregarding what that will to do their love life, sex life, and future overall. And let's not forget about people who think "Baby It's Cold Outside" is rape.

Yes, these people may get 50% of your money, but they live a tortured, miserable existence. And it is because they're insane.

On the other hand you have those who simply aren't leftsits. They are willing to put in the work to earn themselves a good degree and thus a good career. They are willing to put forth the effort to diet and hit the gym and thus have themselves a great looking husband or a great looking wife. They don't look to politics, traits, their race, or their gender to find value, but hone a skill or a craft or a hobby so that they might achieve excellence in one regard or another. If life gets them down or there is some kind of genuine tragedy, they don't immediately crutch to a mental disorder, mired in self-pity, but hit the gym, go running, change their diet, talk to friends, and come back stronger before. And if they breed it's in a stable nuclear family, resulting in stable kids who don't live at home at 32, but go onto become self-supporting adults with their own lives and accomplishments. Yes, all this takes work, effort, rigor, toil, sacrifice, and dedication, but the result is a way better life, a happier life, and to be truthfully honest, we get to bang way hotter people. It's a life leftists will rarely, if ever know, and it's simply because we're sane.

Do not discount the value of sanity today or into the future. 200 years ago such a discussion would be moot because the technology and economic production just wasn't there to provide for all of our basic needs and desires. The harshness of life forced sanity upon people because if they weren't sane, they would die. We simply didn't have the time to think of sanity as a rare or luxurious commodity because it wasn't rare. It was common sense. But now, with economic production allowing for an increasing percentage of the population to live delusional lives, untethered from reality, sanity is not only increasingly rare, but is the only thing that anchors you to what matters most in life - you fellow higher quality human beings. And if you have sanity today, you are a very rich man indeed. I suggest you appreciate your new-found wealth and learn to enjoy the decline.

If you found this interesting please recommend "Sanity is the Future of Wealth" to friends and loved ones. Also check out some of Aaron's other works and sites below!

Consulting: www.assholeconsulting.com
Books: https://www.amazon.com/Aaron-Clarey/e/B00J1ZC350/
Podcast: https://soundcloud.com/aaron-clarey/
Blog: http://captaincapitalism.blogspot.com

Additional books on the following pages.

How Not to Become a Millennial:
A postmortem analysis of the largest sociological disaster in American history – the Millennials – that pulls vital lessons for ALL GENERATIONS to learn.

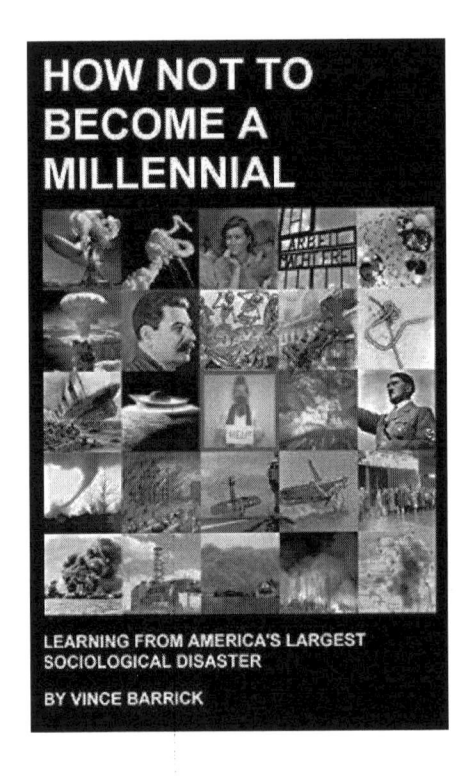

Bachelor Pad Economics:
The financial advice bible for men that address all major and minor financial decisions a man will make from the age of 14 to 74.

Curse of the High IQ:
A book that delves into the maddening problems of being a smart person in a world designed for the common and average.

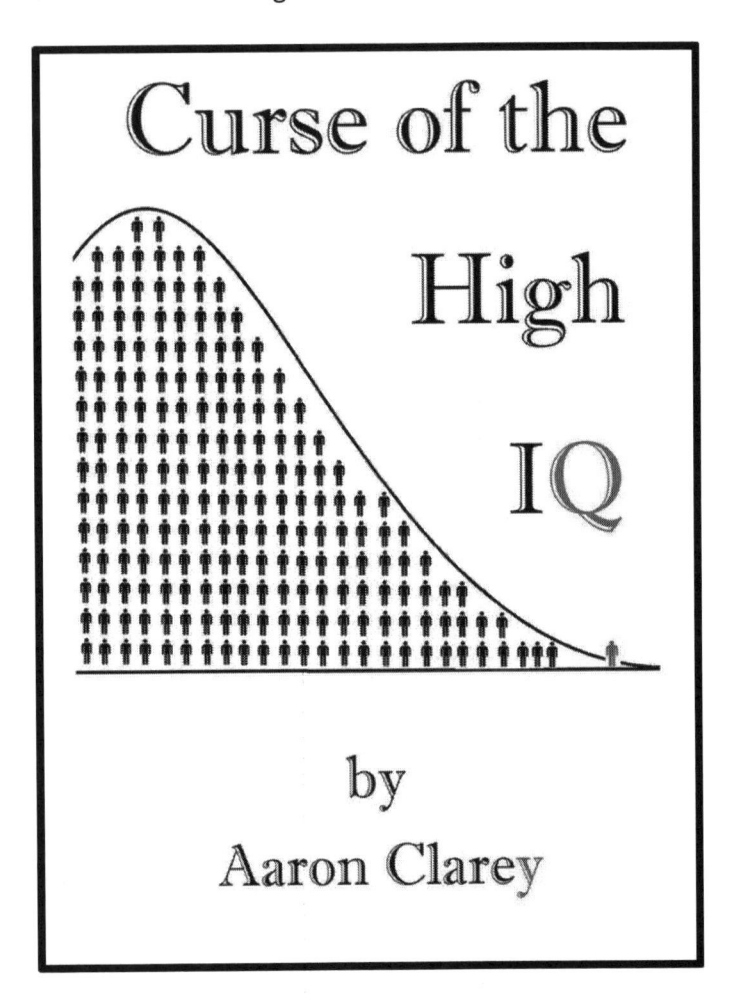

Curse of the High IQ

by
Aaron Clarey

Worthless – The Young Person's Indispensable Guide to Choosing the Right Major:

Make sure you or a loved one doesn't waste 4 years and $100,000 on a worthless degree that will financially cripple you into your 40's.

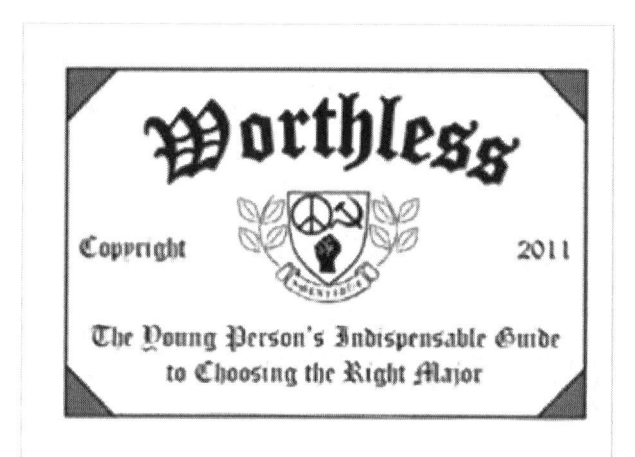

Worthless

Copyright 2011

The Young Person's Indispensable Guide to Choosing the Right Major

By

Aaron Clarey

The Black Man's Guide Out of Poverty:
A sole, single book that has raised more black men out of poverty than all the democrat party ever did.

Poor Richard's Retirement:
Retirement for everyday Americans, especially those who haven't started saving for it yet.

Achieving Minimalism in Theory and Practice – The Key to Success and Happiness in Life

This is a **seminar**, not a book, available through Teachable.com. It is simply designed to get people to spend less than they make. It is *VERY EXPENSIVE*...but so is bankruptcy, student debt, and failing to save for retirement.

Made in the USA
Monee, IL
24 October 2020